LET EVERYTHING THAT HAS BREATH

DEVOTIONAL

Devotions Inspired by the Song

HONOR **HB** BOOKS

Inspiration and Motivation for the Seasons of Life

COOK COMMUNICATIONS MINISTRIES
Colorado Springs, Colorado • Paris, Ontario
KINGSWAY COMMUNICATIONS LTD
Eastbourne, England

Honor® is an imprint of
Cook Communications Ministries, Colorado Springs, CO 80918
Cook Communications, Paris, Ontario
Kingsway Communications, Eastbourne, England

LET EVERYTHING THAT HAS BREATH
© 2006 by Honor Books

Manuscript written by Adam Palmer
Cover Design BMB Design
Cover Photo Credit © #891715 Index Stock Imagery, Inc.
Interior photo © 1997 PhotoSpin

First Printing, 2006
Printed in Canada

        1 2 3 4 5 6 7 8 9 10 Printing/Year 10 09 08 07 06

All Scripture quotations, unless otherwise noted, are taken from the
Holy Bible, New International Version®. *NIV®*. Copyright © 1973,
1978, 1984 by International Bible Society. Used by permission of
Zondervan. All rights reserved. Scripture quotations marked MSG
are taken from *THE MESSAGE.* Copyright © by Eugene H.
Peterson, 1993, 1994, 1995, 1996, 2000, 2001, 2002. Used by permission of NavPress Publishing Group.

ISBN-13: 978-1-56292-811-7
ISBN-10: 1-56292-811-2

LCCN: 2005937826

Introduction

In looking through the Bible, we find that one thing we are instructed to do, over and over again, is to praise the Lord. The word "praise" is mentioned 351 times in the New International Version of the Bible; obviously it is something God feels strongly about.

Why? If we have breath, it is a gift from him. And if we have received that gift, we should praise him for it.

Our gratitude is expressed marvelously in the song "Let Everything That Has Breath" by Matt Redman. This song reminds us of the many ways we are to praise God and the many reasons we have to praise him.

As you walk through these next thirty days with this song, may you gain a glimpse of just why you should praise God. May you gain a new perception of God's worthiness to be praised. May you come to join along with creation and praise him with every breath that is in you.

Let Everything That Has Breath

By Matt Redman

Let everything that, everything that
Everything that has breath praise the Lord
Let everything that, everything that
Everything that has breath praise the Lord

Verse 1:
Praise You in the morning
Praise You in the evening
Praise You when I'm young and when I'm old
Praise You when I'm laughing
Praise You when I'm grieving
Praise You every season of the soul
If we could see how much You're worth
Your power, Your might, Your endless love
Then surely we would never cease to praise

Verse 2:
Praise You in the heavens, joining with the
    angels

Praising You forever and a day
Praise You on the earth now, joining with
    creation
Calling all the nations to Your praise
If they could see how much You're worth
Your power, Your might, Your endless love
Then surely they would never cease to praise

DAY 1: Let Everything That, Everything That Has Breath Praise the Lord

Praise the LORD. Praise God in his sanctuary; praise him in his mighty heavens. Praise him for his acts of power; praise him for his surpassing greatness. Praise him with the sounding of the trumpet, praise him with the harp and lyre, praise him with tambourine and dancing, praise him with the strings and flute, praise him with the clash of cymbals, praise him with resounding cymbals. Let everything that has breath praise the LORD. Praise the LORD.

—PSALM 150:1–6

Praise him for his greatness.

What a band that must be.

Look at the instruments: trumpet, harp, lyre, tambourine, strings, flute, and cymbals. Almost half the band is made up of percussion! Clearly, this is not the kind of band that thrives on terrific instrumentals. It won't be playing any summer festivals for hordes of adoring fans any time soon.

And yet, this is acceptable worship to God. What would probably sound like a whole lot of noise to our untrained ears is wonderful praise to his.

How?

God is just that great. He knows that we could never rival him for imagination or musicality; that's why he just wants some form of praise. It doesn't have to be awesome; it doesn't have to be so great that it would sell millions of copies if it were recorded.

It just has to be honest.

If you're breathing, you can praise God. And you can do it well.

He is great. He is greatly to be praised.

Prayer for the Day:

Dear Lord, thank you for the breath I'm using to pray this prayer right now. Thank you for giving me life. Thank you for giving me breath. Thank you so much for accepting my praise, no matter how it sounds. I do praise you, Lord. I praise you for your acts of power and for your surpassing greatness. I praise you just because you're you. I love you, Lord.

AMEN.

DAY 2: Let Everything That, Everything That Has Breath Praise the Lord

When he came near the place where the road goes down the Mount of Olives, the whole crowd of disciples began joyfully to praise God in loud voices for all the miracles they had seen: "Blessed is the king who comes in the name of the Lord!" "Peace in heaven and glory in the highest!" Some of the Pharisees in the crowd said to Jesus, "Teacher, rebuke your disciples!" "I tell you," he replied, "if they keep quiet, the stones will cry out."

—LUKE 19:37–40

Praise him for his majesty.

Jesus was the rightful King of Israel, and the people who began to praise him in this passage knew it. This act of praise and worship took place just as Jesus was returning to Jerusalem, the capital city of Israel, the place where the king should reside. Jesus was going home.

In their humanness, the disciples welcomed Jesus as a king coming to claim his throne. He was entering Jerusalem in all his majesty. And they were right. In a sense.

But Jesus wasn't entering Jerusalem to lay claim to kingship. Not in the way they were expecting, anyway. His plans were more majestic than

anything they could think up. A suffering king.
A bleeding king. A dying king.

A victorious king.

Jesus entered Jerusalem to high expectations.
And although those expectations weren't met
the way the people imagined, they were indeed
met. And exceeded. Jesus entered Jerusalem
and flipped the perceptions of him on their
collective ears. He changed the world with
one selfless act.

**Jesus entered Jerusalem to the
praises of its people. He left
Jerusalem as their Savior.**

That is true majesty.

Prayer for the Day:

Lord Jesus, you are my King. Right here, right now, I declare it. You are my King. I serve you, Jesus. And I do it because your story compels me to do it. I praise you for your majesty, Jesus, and I pray that you'll remind me of this majestic time in your life. Keep it in front of me, Lord. Let me be a worshipper who appreciates your majesty, Jesus.

AMEN.

DAY 3: Praise You in the Morning

Because of the LORD's great love we are not consumed, for his compassions never fail. They are new every morning; great is your faithfulness.

—LAMENTATIONS 3:22–23

Praise him for his compassion.

Remember the Israelites, wandering through the desert? Remember how God fed them? Manna wafers, found on the ground every morning. They went to bed at night to a perfectly manna-free ground, then woke up with their tents surrounded by the stuff. Every morning, day in and day out without fail, the manna showed up. They would gather what they needed for the day, eat it, and then count on God to provide some for the next day. Which he always did.

It's hard not to think of manna when we read this passage. God's compassions are new every morning. Each morning brings us a fresh, unending supply of God's compassion, God's mercy.

But here's the thing: The manna was good only for that day. If the Israelites tried to hoard it or hang on to it for the next day, it would go bad.

Now, God's compassion never goes bad or spoils, but it is something we should seek each day. Because it's fresh and new each day.

Just like manna.

Prayer for the Day:

Lord, thank you so much for the fresh compassion you've given me today. Thank you for giving me sustenance in my spiritual walk, so that when I fall down, I have the strength to get back up. I'm so grateful that you've chosen to have compassion on me; I pray that I'll be the same way toward others today. I love you, Lord.

AMEN.

DAY 4: Praise You in the Evening

After forty days Noah opened the window he had made in the ark and sent out a raven, and it kept flying back and forth until the water had dried up from the earth. Then he sent out a dove to see if the water had receded from the surface of the ground. But the dove could find no place to set its feet because there was *water over all the surface of the earth; so it returned to Noah in the ark. He reached out his hand and took the dove and brought it back to himself in the ark. He waited seven more days and again sent out the dove from the ark. When the dove returned to him in the evening, there in its beak was a freshly plucked olive leaf! Then Noah knew that the water had receded from the earth.*

—GENESIS 8:6–11

Praise him for new beginnings.

Finally. At long last. The dove had something in its mouth.

Imagine the tension, the nerves that must have been prevalent in the ark just before that dove came back. They'd already sent out a couple of birds to no avail; what would be the difference with this one?

They were never going to get off that ark, were they? They were stuck. Sure, they'd survived the flood, but how long was it going to take for these floodwaters to recede, anyway? They'd lost track of the days they'd been on board. They were going stir crazy.

And then there it was. The dove. And the olive branch.

Hope at last.

Can you fathom the celebration they had in that ark? We do a little jig when we're done with a ten-hour road trip. They'd been cooped up on the ark for way, way, way longer than that—just over one year (370 days). There was definitely some praising going on that evening.

God's timeline doesn't always line up with ours; and though we'd often like to get all the answers first thing in the morning, sometimes it takes a little while for the dove to get back to the ship, so to speak.

But God is always in control, no matter what time of day.

Praise him in the evening.

Prayer for the Day:

God, sometimes I have a tough time waiting until evening to hear from you. I admit that I, at times, want my prayers answered the second I'm done praying them. Help me to enjoy the day, whether I have answers or not. Help me to trust you today—and tomorrow—so that I might bring glory to your name.

Amen.

DAY 5: Praise You When I'm Young

But Samuel was ministering before the LORD—a boy wearing a linen ephod. Each year his mother made him a little robe and took it to him when she went up with her husband to offer the annual sacrifice. Eli would bless Elkanah and his wife, saying, "May the LORD give you children by this woman to take the place of the one she prayed for and gave to the LORD." Then they would go home. And the LORD was gracious to Hannah; she conceived and gave birth to three sons and two daughters. Meanwhile, the boy Samuel grew up in the presence of the LORD.

—1 SAMUEL 2:18–21

Praise him for his goodness.

It's amazing how sensitive children are to God. Children's church workers know this firsthand; there's not much worship more pure and honest than that of little kids as they worship God. Eyes closed, hands raised, singing at the top of their lungs, children's innocent worship is more authentic than that of most of the adults singing in the main sanctuary at the same time.

Samuel was a kid like that—a kid who was extremely sensitive to God. Before he was born, his mother, Hannah, just couldn't get pregnant. She prayed and promised that if God would give her a child, she would give the child over to his service. It wasn't long before Samuel was born, and it wasn't long after that he was serving in the temple.

No matter how old we get, we can still look for and long for the honest, pure, innocent worship of our youth. Then we, like Samuel, can continue to grow up in the presence of the Lord, worshipping and praising him without the cares of adulthood.

When we can let go of our fears and restraints, and trust his goodness, then we will find ourselves ministering to God just like Samuel did. Because God is so good to us.

Prayer for the Day:

God, thank you for your goodness. I'm sorry for the times I don't believe in it, whether consciously or unconsciously. I pray that you'll help me to worship you like a child, Lord. All-out, no-holds-barred worship. Let me hold nothing back, God. It's all yours, anyway. Help me to trust your goodness. I love you.

AMEN.

DAY 6: And When I'm Old

When David had fled and made his escape, he went to Samuel at Ramah and told him all that Saul had done to him. Then he and Samuel went to Naioth and stayed there. Word came to Saul: "David is in Naioth at Ramah"; so he sent men to capture him. But when they saw a group of prophets prophesying, with Samuel standing there as their leader, the Spirit of God came upon Saul's men and they also prophesied. Saul was told about it, and he sent more men, and they prophesied too. Saul sent men a third time, and they also prophesied. Finally, he himself left for Ramah and went to the great cistern at Secu. And he asked, "Where are

Samuel and David?" "Over in Naioth at Ramah," they said. So Saul went to Naioth at Ramah. But the Spirit of God came even upon him, and he walked along prophesying until he came to Naioth. He stripped off his robes and also prophesied in Samuel's presence. He lay that way all that day and night. This is why people say, "Is Saul also among the prophets?"

—1 Samuel 19:18–24

Praise him for his presence.

Yesterday we read that Samuel grew up in the presence of the Lord. That lasted until he was an old man.

Today we rejoin Samuel in his old age, in the last story the Bible has to tell about him before he dies. Saul, the God-rejected king of Israel, was intently pursuing David in order to kill him. David escaped one of Saul's attempts and took refuge with Samuel for a short time.

Saul heard about the hiding place, though, and sent some men to apprehend David. Nothing doing. As the men got close to Samuel, the presence of God was so thick that they couldn't do anything but worship. Their efforts to obtain David were ineffectual.

So Saul decided to take on the mission himself, but the same thing happened to him.

That was some serious power enveloping our friend Samuel. But it didn't come overnight. It came only as Samuel spent his lifetime seeking to live in the presence of God.

Fortunately for us, we don't have to be temple priests like Samuel in order to dwell in God's presence. Thanks to the work of Jesus on the cross, the presence of God already resides in us.

This powerful presence is something God has chosen to share with us. Praise him for it.

Prayer for the Day:

Wow, God. This is humbling, to think of your presence residing within me. It's just amazing, Lord. Thank you for choosing me. Thank you for allowing me to worship and praise you. Thank you for your presence, God. I pray that I would walk in your presence today and that it would spill out onto the people I encounter. I love you, Lord.

AMEN.

DAY 7: Praise You When I'm Laughing

Then the LORD said, "I will surely return to you about this time next year, and Sarah your wife will have a son." Now Sarah was listening at the entrance to the tent, which was behind him. Abraham and Sarah were already old and well advanced in years, and Sarah was past the age of childbearing. So Sarah laughed to herself as she thought, "After I am worn out and my *master is old, will I now have this pleasure?" Then the L*ORD* said to Abraham, "Why did Sarah laugh and say, 'Will I really have a child, now that I am old?' Is anything too hard for the L*ORD*? I will return to you at the appointed time next year and Sarah will have a son."*

—GENESIS **18:10–14**

Praise him for his promises.

Let's get a little perspective here. Especially in the part of this passage that says, "Abraham and Sarah were already old and well advanced in years." That's putting it mildly. Abraham was ninety-nine years old and Sarah was ninety.

No wonder Sarah laughed so incredulously. God's promise to give her a child by the age of ninety-one sounded ridiculous to her, especially when he'd not yet delivered on his original promise to Abraham. (See Gen. 15:5.)

But God was true to his word, and a year later, he brought Sarah genuine, laughing praise when he finally delivered a baby boy to her and

Abraham. Just as he had promised. It was then that Sarah said, "God has brought me laughter, and everyone who hears about this will laugh with me" (Gen. 21:6).

And to seal the deal, Abraham and Sarah named this miracle child "Isaac," which means "laughter." So every time they called his name, they remembered that they were praising God in their laughter.

God is a God of joy and laughter. No, things aren't always rosy in life, but when we remember God's promises to us—to care for us and never to leave us—we can still walk through this life praising God for his promises, laughing all the way.

Prayer for the Day:

God, you're so good. And you're true to your word. Thank you for your promises, Lord. Thank you for what you've said you will do for me, to me, and through me. I do trust your promises, and I praise you for them. I know they will be fulfilled in your time, not mine.

AMEN.

DAY 8: Praise You When I'm Laughing

And Mary said: "My soul glorifies the Lord and my spirit rejoices in God my Savior, for he has been mindful of the humble state of his servant."

—LUKE 1:46–48

Praise him for his joy.

Sarah laughed; Mary rejoiced.

Another improbable mother, another miracle baby, another promise from God fulfilled. Of course, that's just the way he works. Except this time, his promise wasn't just to Mary—it was to the people of Israel.

God had promised he would send a Redeemer—a Messiah—to the Israelites, and, like Sarah, they were growing impatient with all the waiting. But he did it according to his own timing, and when he finally sent Jesus, there was indeed some rejoicing from Mary, the woman who would give birth to the Christ. The Savior of the world. A baby. She would be responsible for this God-child. She would bring him into the world. She would raise him. And she would one day see him die for all of mankind.

Rejoicing.

It's hard to imagine what went through Mary's mind, but she was definitely happy. Even in the face of the overwhelming responsibility God had given her, she was joyful. She could've frozen under that weight. She could've freaked out. But she didn't.

She got happy.

God's joy is always available for us, even when the circumstances of life threaten to make us numb. And so we can always praise him in our laughter. Because he's the one who provides the laughter in the first place.

Prayer for the Day:

God, you're awesome. Amazing. Astounding. I can't even begin to comprehend your ways, Lord. I don't know how you do it, but you provide joy, even in the face of tremendous obstacles. Thank you for giving me responsibilities in this world; thank you for helping me carry those responsibilities. I pray that I would bring glory to your name in everything I do. I love you.

AMEN.

DAY 9: Praise You When I'm Grieving

Jesus, once more deeply moved, came to the tomb. It was a cave with a stone laid across the entrance. "Take away the stone," he said. "But, Lord," said Martha, the sister of the dead man, "by this time there is a bad odor, for he has been there four days." Then Jesus said, "Did I not tell you that if you believed, you would see the glory of God?" So they took away the stone. Then Jesus looked *up and said, "Father, I thank you that you have heard me. I knew that you always hear me, but I said this for the benefit of the people standing here, that they may believe that you sent me." When he had said this, Jesus called in a loud voice, "Lazarus, come out!" The dead man came out, his hands and feet wrapped with strips of linen, and a cloth around his face. Jesus said to them, "Take off the grave clothes and let him go."*

—JOHN 11:38–44

Praise him for his perspective.

Lazarus was there. Inside the tomb. Dead. And it was Jesus' fault.

See, Jesus had gotten a message some days earlier that Lazarus was sick. Jesus was out of town at the time, and instead of hurrying to Lazarus's side to heal him, he took his time getting there. On purpose. He was going to use this event to teach his disciples a lesson.

Finally, Jesus and his disciples arrived in Bethany, the hometown of Lazarus, and they found Lazarus already dead and buried. The people there, including Lazarus's sisters, had already given up hope.

They didn't have Jesus' perspective.

He saw things a little differently. This was all part of the plan, a setup for something grand. Their grief would soon be turned into something completely different, because Jesus knew how it would end.

When we experience grief, it's difficult to maintain Jesus' perspective. But we must remember that God sees everything from his own perspective. He sees the whole picture while we only have glimpses; he has the last word while we only have a few letters here and there.

And yet, Jesus wept. He empathizes with us, even in his omniscience. We can praise him, because he is a God of perspective— both his and ours.

Prayer for the Day:

Jesus, thank you for your perspective. Thank you for looking at things through my eyes. You understand why I feel the way I feel, even though you know I sometimes don't have a right to feel that way. I praise you in the midst of my grief, because you know something I don't. Remind me of your perspective, Lord.

AMEN.

DAY 10: Praise You When I'm Grieving

After Nathan had gone home, the LORD struck the child that Uriah's wife had borne to David, and he became ill. David pleaded with God for the child. He fasted and went into his house and spent the nights lying on the ground. The elders of his household stood beside him to get him up from the ground, but he refused, and he would not eat any food with them. On the seventh day the child died. David's servants were afraid to tell him that the child was dead, for they thought, "While the child was still living, we spoke to David but he would not listen to us. How can we tell him the child is dead? He may do something desperate." David noticed that his servants were *whispering among themselves and he realized the child was dead. "Is the child dead?" he asked. "Yes," they replied, "he is dead." Then David got up from the ground. After he had washed, put on lotions and changed his clothes, he went into the house of the L*ORD *and worshiped. Then he went to his own house, and at his request they served him food, and he ate. His servants asked him, "Why are you acting this way? While the child was alive, you fasted and wept, but now that the child is dead, you get up and eat!" He answered, "While the child was still alive, I fasted and wept. I thought, 'Who knows? The L*ORD *may be gracious to me and let the child live.' But now that he is dead, why should I fast? Can I bring him back again? I will go to him, but he will not return to me." Then David comforted his wife Bathsheba, and he went to her and lay with her. She gave birth to a son, and they named him Solomon.*

—2 SAMUEL 12:15–24

Praise him for his eternal greatness.

Wow. Is David a cold, distant, emotionally starved man or what? It sure seems like it, doesn't it?

But let's back up and examine this story in a little more depth. If you look at the first verse, you see that the child is referred to as the one "Uriah's wife had borne to David." This was a baby conceived in adultery—the result of a sinful act. King David was at home when he should've been at war; he saw the lovely Bathsheba, sinned with her, and then discovered she was pregnant. To cover it up, he had Bathsheba's husband, Uriah, killed. He then married Bathsheba in order to pass the baby off as his own.

How's that for cold and distant?

But here's the thing. David was found out and exposed, and he realized he had blown it. Big time. He was highly repentant, and God had mercy on both him and Bathsheba, but the child from their adulterous union did not survive.

David understood that God is eternally great, that this life is but a flash, but that God's greatness lasts and lasts and lasts outside of time. David was mature enough to understand that God was still God, even in the midst of his suffering.

God is not limited to our finite amount of time on this earth—he is eternal. And he is great. And it is for this that we are to praise him.

Prayer for the Day:

God, I admit I just don't understand the concept of you existing outside of time. Eternity is such a difficult thing to grasp. Nevertheless, I believe you are eternal. I believe you are eternally great. I pray you'll make this real to me, God. I can't even come close to comprehending it without your help.

AMEN.

DAY 11:
Praise You Every Season of the Soul

As long as the earth endures, seedtime and harvest, cold and heat, summer and winter, day and night will never cease.

—GENESIS 8:22

Praise him for his steadfastness.

Seasons are just a part of life. Some of us live in places where seasons rarely change—the weather is always hot or always cold. But even where the weather doesn't change, there are still seasons. We may celebrate Christmas in eighty-degree weather, but we're still celebrating Christmas.

The point is this: God set up the seasons. They were his idea, these ever-changing givers of variety. The snowy, dead winter always gives way to the blossoms of spring; the heat of summer always gives way to the crisp chill of autumn. These seasons have gone on year after year after year, long before any of us got here, and they'll continue to do so long after we leave this earth.

And these seasons are marvelous pictures of the soul, which goes through seasons itself. Sometimes we find ourselves buried in dreary spiritual snow, longing to see the sun again. But those barren seasons always give way to times of spiritual refreshment and newness. Sometimes we feel spiritually dry and burnt, like a too-hot summer day that saps the energy out of us the moment we go outside. But that season of our soul always gives way, eventually, to a brisk, colorful autumn.

Despite the changing seasons of our lives, we must continue to praise God. Just as the sun rises and sets and the earth goes through its motions regardless of the seasons, so we must also purpose in our hearts to praise God without fail.

The seasons change, but God doesn't. He remains steadfast for all time.

Prayer for the Day:

Lord God, I praise you for your steadfastness. It's so amazing, God, that you remain so thoroughly good throughout all the changing seasons I encounter. I'm so thankful for your steadfast character. Teach me to rely on it daily, Lord.

AMEN.

DAY 12:
If We Could See How Much You're Worth

We do, however, speak a message of wisdom among the mature, but not the wisdom of this age or of the rulers of this age, who are coming to nothing. No, we speak of God's secret wisdom, a wisdom that has been hidden and that God destined for our glory before time began. None of the rulers of this age understood it, for if they had, they would not have crucified the Lord of glory. However, as it is written: "No eye has seen, no ear has heard, no mind has conceived what God has prepared for those who love him."

—1 Corinthians 2:6–9

Praise him for his mystery.

In the time-honored and beloved film *A Christmas Story*, little Ralphie Parker is ecstatic about receiving his Radio Orphan Annie decoder pin in the mail. Orphan Annie has a message for Ralphie, and he's been waiting forever to get this special decoder pin in the mail.

It's a great scene. The package arrives, and Ralphie enthusiastically takes the decoder pin straight upstairs and locks himself in the bathroom. He reaches for the secret message paper containing the secret message from Radio Orphan Annie, written directly to him, Ralphie Parker! He methodically works the code, carefully writing down each letter of the cipher as he gets it. Finally, his job done, he sits back to read this all-important message from Radio Orphan Annie: "Be sure to drink your Ovaltine!"

Sometimes life feels like that, doesn't it? You experience a buildup of tension and suspense in anticipating something, only to feel let down when the secret or mystery wasn't nearly as mysterious as you'd expected.

If only we could catch a glimpse of what God was trying to say to us. If only we could get as excited about his words, his mystery, as Ralphie was about that Radio Orphan Annie decoder pin. If only.

But what if we decided to praise God for his mystery? For the fact that we don't have him figured out? Radio Orphan Annie was just promoting a vitamin drink; God's promises are the real deal. He delivers.

It is exactly this part of God that makes him worth knowing. If only we could see that about him. What would that do to the way we look at him?

Prayer for the Day:

God, you are mysterious. Maybe I've never really thought of this before, but I think I'm fascinated by your mystery, Lord. I pray that you would reveal yourself to me anew, God. That you would show me something about yourself I don't already know. I want to be captivated by you, God.

AMEN.

DAY 13: Your Power

And a woman was there who had been subject to bleeding for twelve years, but no one could heal her. She came up behind him and touched the edge of his cloak, and immediately her bleeding stopped. "Who touched me?" Jesus asked. When they all denied it, Peter said, "Master, the people are crowding and pressing against you." But Jesus said, "Someone touched me; I know that power has gone out from me." Then the woman, seeing that she could not go unnoticed, came trembling and fell at his feet. In the presence of all the people, she told why she had touched him and how she had been instantly healed. Then he said to her, "Daughter, your faith has healed you. Go in peace."

—Luke 8:43–48

Praise him for his natural power.

Power. We're used to it, aren't we? When we plug in a toaster, we don't hope it works. We just expect it to make our bread warm and crispy, end of story. In fact, most of us take power for granted—until it's knocked out by a storm, and then we realize how much we rely on it.

But usually, it's just there for us to use. All we have to do is plug in and we're ready to go.

That is what this woman thought about Jesus. That's the type of faith she had in his healing power. She knew that if she could just touch even the tip of his cloak, she'd get results. Simple as that. She just wanted to plug into Jesus' power.

Because healing was natural for him. Literally. It was part of his nature. And this woman believed that so deeply that touching Jesus' clothes made as much sense to her as plugging in a toaster does to us. It just goes without saying that there is power there.

All that remains is for us to plug in.

Prayer for the Day:

Jesus, you're powerful. Full of power. It's in your nature to have power, but sometimes I forget that. I forget how powerful you are, and I get a little overwhelmed by the things the world throws at me. Forgive me for that, Lord. Help me to trust your power.

AMEN.

DAY 14:
Your Might

But Moses sought the favor of the LORD his God. "O LORD," he said, "why should your anger burn against your people, whom you brought out of Egypt with great power and a mighty hand?"

—EXODUS 32:11

Praise him for his mighty, delivering hand.

Let's take a look at what God's mighty hand threw at Egypt in order to get the Israelites out of there:

He turned the Nile River into blood.

He covered the land with frogs.

He turned the dust of the ground into gnats.

He sent thick swarms of flies into Egypt.

He made the Egyptian livestock sick, which led to their death.

He sent festering boils onto the men and animals of Egypt.

He sent a blistering hailstorm that severely damaged the land.

He sent swarms of locusts to eat everything that was left.

He made the sky so dark no one could see.

He killed every firstborn son in Egypt.

He parted the Red Sea, let the Israelites walk across, then drowned Pharaoh's army in it.

That is some serious might.

In today's passage, all these things are wrapped up in the word "mighty," a word Moses uses in trying to dissuade God from wiping out the Israelites for worshipping a false god, the golden calf.

The Israelites had forgotten about God's mighty hand, but Moses sure hadn't. He remembered it well. Moses knew what God was capable of, and he wanted to make sure that God's mighty hand blessed Israel instead of cursing it.

How well do we remember what God's mighty, delivering hand is capable of? He is mighty, and he is worthy to be praised.

Prayer for the Day:

God, your might is amazing. Your power is awe inspiring. I'm truly sorry for the times I forget about your might. And what's humbling is that you still seek out a relationship with me. I praise you for your might, Lord, and I'm so thankful that you love me.

AMEN.

DAY 15: Your Endless Love

GOD's works are so great, worth a lifetime of study—endless enjoyment! Splendor and beauty mark his craft; his generosity never gives out. His miracles are his memorial—this GOD of Grace, this GOD of Love.

—PSALM 111:2–4 MSG

Praise him for his endless love.

What does the phrase "endless love" mean to you? What pops into your mind when you hear that phrase? Wedding vows? Seventy-fifth anniversary celebrations? Perhaps a departed spouse, parent, or child?

When we think of "endless love," we tend to think of romantic love or perhaps familial love. Or perhaps we think of the platonic love we share with best friends.

God's love, though, is endless; but it is also beginning-less. God's love for us has no beginning or end. It just is.

Like the air that surrounds us, God's love is just there, with no real perceivable beginning or ending. Yes, we know the atmosphere does have an ending, somewhere up in the sky, but we cannot see it. We cannot even perceive it while we breathe. We simply inhale, and there it is. Just like God's love.

In full supply, without beginning and without end. Full of splendor. Beautiful. Generous.

We could devote a lifetime to studying God's love and still not comprehend it. But we can receive it all the while, for it is endless.

Prayer for the Day:

God, thank you for your endless love. Thank you for loving me even when I was unlovable. Thank you for seeing fit to search me out with your all-encompassing love. Thank you for giving me the ability to breathe it in. I'm so in love with you, God.

AMEN.

DAY 16:
Then Surely We Would Never Cease to Praise

There was also a prophetess, Anna, the daughter of Phanuel, of the tribe of Asher. She was very old; she had lived with her husband seven years after her marriage, and then was a widow until she was eighty-four. She never left the temple but worshiped night and day, fasting and praying. Coming up to them at that very moment, she gave thanks to God and spoke about the child to all who were looking forward to the redemption of Jerusalem.

—LUKE 2:36–38

Praise him for his dedication.

Anna was one dedicated woman. Because women generally got married very young in ancient Israel, we can assume that Anna did the same. Seven years later, her husband died and she became a widow. So she was still pretty young.

And what did she do? She decided to hang out at the temple until the age of eighty-four. Eighty-four!

This is a woman who essentially spent her adult life worshipping God. She was consumed by the Lord and by everything he had to offer. She was fully, completely dedicated to his purposes.

And he was dedicated to her. How else would she have been able to sustain her worship regimen if she wasn't getting anything in return? God sustained her in her worship, because of his dedication to her.

Anna had been waiting around in the hope of catching a glimpse of the Messiah, and God rewarded her dedication with the honor of being one of two witnesses to the young Christ.

When we worship God, we are dedicating ourselves to him, and he returns the favor and dedicates himself to us. We may not know exactly how or when we will see physical examples of that dedication, but we can rest in the knowledge that, even if we get as old as Anna, we'll see God's dedication someday.

Prayer for the Day:

Lord, thank you for your dedication to me. If I really understood it, God, I think I would literally never stop worshipping you. As it is, I like to worship and praise you, because you are worthy of it. Draw me closer to you, Lord. Help me to be more dedicated to you, just like you're dedicated to me.

AMEN.

DAY 17: Praise You in the Heavens

The heavens praise your wonders, O LORD, your faithfulness too, in the assembly of the holy ones. For who in the skies above can compare with the LORD? Who is like the LORD among the heavenly beings?

—PSALM 89:5–6

Praise him for his faithfulness.

What is there in the sky that can compare with the Lord? If you really want to make an accurate comparison, drive across Kansas in the spring, when the weather fronts are active and the flatlands enable you to see for miles in any direction. With that perspective you will gain a whole new appreciation for the sky. Shockingly blue during the day, filled with pinprick starlight at night, the sky is indeed amazing. Miles and miles of God's handiwork, on display for us to see. Even in rainy weather, the sky takes on a new dimension, subtly textured and almost rhythmic with clouds.

Take a look at the sky. What do you see? Look at it with new eyes, the eyes of a child. Look at it as if you've never seen it before. Allow yourself to be taken in by its beauty. It's always there above us, yet we often forget about it or take it for granted.

Are you finished staring yet? Can you tear yourself away from the wondrous view?

God dwarfs it. There is nothing in the sky that even comes close to comparing to him. He is faithful to us in ways we could never imagine. The sky is magnificent, yes, and parts of it can remind us of God, give us glimpses of him; but in a side-by-side comparison of grandeur, wonder, and faithfulness, the sky loses hands down.

Praise him for his faithfulness. Praise him in the heavens.

Prayer for the Day:

Lord, I look into the heavens and see them praising you. I see your creation singing your praise simply by its very existence. I can't imagine what you must be like, really, in all your glory. But I still look forward to finding out, little by little, starting today.

AMEN.

DAY 18: Joining with the Angels

Then I looked and heard the voice of many angels, numbering thousands upon thousands, and ten thousand times ten thousand. They encircled the throne and the living creatures and the elders. In a loud voice they sang: "Worthy is the Lamb, who was slain, to receive power and wealth and wisdom and strength and honor and glory and praise!" Then I heard every creature in heaven and on earth and under the earth and on the sea, and all that is in them, singing: "To him who sits on the throne and to the Lamb be praise and honor and glory and power, for ever and ever!"

—REVELATION 5:11–13

Praise him for his position.

The angels have it right, don't they? They know what's up—who really should be praised.

Angels are magnificent creations, and when they appear in the Bible, they usually have to reassure the person to whom they are appearing not to be afraid. There's just something about angels that strikes awe and fright into anyone who sees them.

So here are these angels—mighty, powerful beings—and what do they do? Do they try to appropriate any worship for themselves, spectacular as they are? No way. They have their priorities in order.

But why? Why do these angels join together singing praises to Jesus? Because of his position. He is the Lamb who was slain; he is the one on the eternal throne. He's the one deserving of praise because of his position.

Today's passage gives us a snapshot of heaven. This is what it's like there; this is an idea of how we'll spend part of eternity. Praising the God who rescued us from death and hell, praising the One who paid for our entry into heaven.

He is in the position to be praised. The angels know it. So should we.

Prayer for the Day:

Lord, to tell you the truth, I'm a little bit humbled here. Sometimes I forget that I'm not the center of the universe; you are. It's so easy to get wrapped up in my own life and to shoulder you out, but if ten thousand angels see it as important to praise you, maybe I should give you a little more importance in my life. Please forgive me, Lord, and help me to look in your direction always.

AMEN.

DAY 19: Praise You in the Heavens, Joining with the Angels

Praise the LORD. Praise the LORD from the heavens, praise him in the heights above. Praise him, all his angels, praise him, all his heavenly hosts. Praise him, sun and moon, praise him, all you shining stars. Praise him, you highest heavens and you waters above the skies. Let them praise the name of the LORD, for he commanded and they were created.

—PSALM 148:1–5

Praise him for his imagination.

Have you ever looked at a new invention and thought, *This is really cool. Who could've thought of this—let alone made it a reality?* Portable music players. Velcro. Teflon. That knife that can cut through both a shoe and a tomato. The list goes on and on.

History has seen imagination-filled invention after imagination-filled invention. Some have stuck with us (vulcanized rubber tires); others have faded into the mists of time (toaster french fries). But all have one thing in common: They're nothing compared to what God has imagined.

This psalm pretty much nails it. The sun, the moon, the stars ... the highest points of the sky, the depths of the oceans. God thought it all up. He created all that variety, all that contrasting wonder.

And yet, this God who made the sky, the seas, and everything in between chooses to commune with us, his greatest creation. Is there any question, then, that we should choose to join with the angels and praise him?

Prayer for the Day:

Lord, I'm in awe of the things you've done. You created the entire world and everything in it. You made me. You made a way for me to spend eternity with you. You've done everything for me. I praise you, Lord, and I'm so thankful for your imagination. Help me to appreciate your wonderful inventiveness.

AMEN.

DAY 20: Praising You Forever and a Day

The fear of the Lord is the beginning of wisdom; all who follow his precepts have good understanding. To him belongs eternal praise.

—Psalm 111:10

Praise him for his unending gift of wisdom.

It's nice to receive gifts, isn't it? Who among us doesn't like a nice little present every now and then?

And what better present is there than wisdom?

God promises to give us wisdom; in today's passage we see where that wisdom comes from. It comes from keeping God in proper perspective.

The psalmist wrote that fearing the Lord is the beginning of wisdom. That doesn't mean we are to be afraid of him. Rather, it means that we need to show him deference and respect. That, while we tremble at his wildness, we can also take comfort in his goodness.

The psalmist then wrote that when we follow God's precepts—his laws—we have good understanding. See, God knows what he's doing; he knows what we need and, more important, what we don't need. When we study his Word, we can have a wisdom and understanding that go beyond anything we could come up with on our own.

And, for that reason, the psalmist says, we are to give God eternal praise.

Eternal praise in exchange for eternal wisdom. Sounds like a great gift.

Prayer for the Day:

Father God, I thank you for your gift of wis-
dom, found in your Scriptures. I thank you for
your love toward me, that you even offer me
wisdom. I praise you for it, Lord. I pray that
you'll help me to look at you—and my life—
wisely, to operate and live in such a way that I
bring glory to your name. I thank you and
praise you.

Amen.

DAY 21: Praising You Forever and a Day

All this is for your benefit, so that the grace that is reaching more and more people may cause thanksgiving to overflow to the glory of God. Therefore we do not lose heart. Though outwardly we are wasting away, yet inwardly we are being renewed day by day. For our light and momentary troubles are achieving for us an eternal glory that far outweighs them all.

—2 Corinthians 4:15–17

Praise him for his renewing grace.

Have you ever had a bad day? Not just a regular bad day, but a terrible, awful, horrible, "completely baffling how this day got to be so bad" day? The kind of day when you hope to go to bed early just to have the day behind you, because you know there's no way the next day could be any worse?

Perhaps today was that kind of day. Perhaps you're still carrying the painful memory of a day like that, even though it was days, months, or years ago.

The crazy thing is that, according to the Bible, days like that are "light and momentary troubles."

Light and momentary! How is that even possible? This is heavy stuff, a major weight on the shoulders. This is the worst day ever. There's no way it's "light and momentary."

Except that God says it is. Because he's offering us a continual, renewing grace that outweighs anything we might encounter in this life. It's a grace that reaches others and that ultimately points us toward an eternal glory that will make all our hard days here on earth vanish as if they'd never happened.

We may have a difficult day—or even a difficult life—here on earth, but it is no match for the grandeur and glory that await us in heaven.

Praise him forever for his renewing grace.

Prayer for the Day:

Jesus, thank you for providing grace for me. Thank you for coming to this earth. Thank you for dying. Thank you for having the worst day anyone in history has ever had. You came through on the other side of it, so I know I can be encouraged in that. Help me to grasp this concept of eternal glory so that I can make it through the rough times I have here in this world. I love you, Lord.

AMEN.

DAY 22: Praise You on the Earth Now

Like your name, O God, your praise reaches to the ends of the earth; your right hand is filled with righteousness.

—PSALM 48:10

Praise him for his omnipresence.

Colin C. Smith is an artist from Omaha, Nebraska. He works in a unique style that involves aluminum, stencils, professional-size paint sprayers, signage, and oblique pop-culture references. He melds traditional and technological elements to create layered, colorful art that has both depth and sheen.

Colin's pieces of art were once displayed in a small art gallery, a modest, white-walled space that was sparse in nature. Colin's work dominated the landscape of the gallery, and there was nothing on the walls that wasn't his. Piece after piece, painting after painting—it was all Colin's.

In essence, there wasn't a part of that gallery that didn't have Colin's signature style somewhere on it.

Take a look at our earth. Our God is a unique God, and there isn't a part of our earth that doesn't have his signature on it. His handiwork is everywhere, reaching to the ends of the earth.

His righteousness knows no boundaries. There is nowhere to hide from it; there is no fence to keep it out.

God is omnipresent, and in that we can take solace. There is no place on this earth he can't reach. He can touch us anywhere we are.

Prayer for the Day:

How comforting that is, God. I'm so glad that you can find me anywhere I might be. You never leave me, you never forsake me, and even when I feel like I'm in a place you can't go, you're still there. Thank you for rescuing me; thank you for reaching me. I love you.

AMEN.

DAY 23: Joining with Creation

Shout with joy to God, all the earth! Sing the glory of his name; make his praise glorious! Say to God, "How awesome are your deeds! So great is your power that your enemies cringe before you. All the earth bows down to you; they sing praise to you, they sing praise to your name."

—Psalm 66:1–4

Praise him for his inclusiveness.

Little Alex was most certainly not a born soccer player. Yes, he was only six years old, and this was his first time to be on a team, but even in practice, everyone knew he wasn't gifted like some of the other kids on the team. He was more interested in putting clumps of grass into his mouth than in locating the ball, much less kicking it.

But he was on the team, and that meant he had to play. In the five- and six-year-old leagues, all the kids had to play, no matter how uninterested in the sport they were. When game day arrived, Alex sat out the first few minutes, but eventually he heard his name called. He strapped on some shin guards and went out on to the field, fully prepared to do nothing.

Play resumed, and Alex stood around looking a little bewildered. At that age, the kids don't really play positions very well; most of them go for the ball all at the same time. The bunch approached Alex, and suddenly the ball squirted out from the bunch right toward him.

The next thing he knew, he was streaking toward the goal. Little Alex, the unwanted, the untalented, the uninterested, was about to score.

God understands this sort of inclusiveness. He knows more about us than we know about ourselves. He has a plan for us, and part of that plan involves us getting into the game, joining with his creation in singing praise to his name.

The entire earth bows before him; we should as well. He's given us the ability.

Prayer for the Day:

Jesus, I love you. Thank you for including me in your plans. Thank you for letting me join the earth in singing your praise. I do praise you; I do worship you. Thank you for putting me on your team. Thank you for encouraging me to get in the game.

AMEN.

DAY 24: Praise You on the Earth Now, Joining with Creation

May his name endure forever; may it continue as long as the sun. All nations will be blessed through him, and they will call him blessed. Praise be to the LORD God, the God of Israel, who alone does marvelous deeds. Praise be to his glorious name forever; may the whole earth be filled with his glory. Amen and Amen.

—PSALM 72:17–19

Praise him for his marvelous deeds.

What's the greatest thing you've ever done? Is there even a list in your mind of great things you've done, or do you see yourself only as a failure? What in your life will endure the tests of time, and what has been a mere flicker?

These are hard questions, the type of questions that creep up on us in the quiet moments when we take a break from the busyness of our lives and ponder the future. We tend to wonder what sort of mark we'll leave on the world, what our legacy will be.

Fortunately, we serve a God who has the greatest legacy we could ever imagine. Unlike us, his name will endure forever. He is the only one to do marvelous deeds. Our greatest deeds look woefully small next to his greatest deeds. And the earth—all 510,065,284.702 square kilometers of it—is full of his glory.

God is great and is greatly to be praised.

Prayer for the Day:

God, you really blow my mind. I'm just awestruck at how great you are. Your deeds are marvelous; your creation is full of your glory. I'm just glad I get to join in with the praise of your creation, that I get to add my voice to the sound track. I love you so much, Lord.

AMEN.

DAY 25:
Calling All the Nations to Your Praise

But he took note of their distress when he heard their cry; for their sake he remembered his covenant and out of his great love he relented. He caused them to be pitied by all who held them captive. Save us, O LORD our God, and gather us from the nations, that we may give thanks to your holy name and glory in your praise.

—PSALM 106:44–47

Praise him for his covenant remembrance.

This psalm is a psalm of deliverance—of mercy and grace. The thirty-eight verses that precede these are a laundry list of almost every sin the Israelites had committed up to that point. It is a list of every reason God could possibly have not to help them.

And then notice these words: "For their sake he remembered his covenant and out of his great love he relented." God had all sorts of reasons not to help the Israelites in the time of their distress, but he had an even greater reason to ignore those reasons: the covenant he'd made with them.

God is a God of his word. When he promises something, he delivers. When he makes a covenant, he keeps it, even if we don't. His people were spread across the nations, and as they cried out to God, they knew he would hear them even scattered across the known world. Their praise of him from the different nations would reach him. All would be forgiven; their praise would be accepted.

There's nothing we can do to make God forget his covenant. We could be scattered to any nation, our backs fully turned to God, and even then, should we turn around and offer praise or cry out to him, he will hear it. It is in his nature.

He will never forget us.

Prayer for the Day:

God, I don't have the best memory sometimes. I forget things; we all do. Thanks for remembering me. Thank you for turning your ear toward me, Lord, so that when I call on you, you hear me. Thank you for your great love that outweighs my stubbornness, my sin. I'm so grateful, Lord.

AMEN.

DAY 26:
If They Could See How Much You're Worth

When Jesus came to the region of Caesarea Philippi, he asked his disciples, "Who do people say the Son of Man is?" They replied, "Some say John the Baptist; others say Elijah; and still others, Jeremiah or one of the prophets." "But what about you?" he asked. "Who do you say I am?" Simon Peter answered, "You are the Christ, the Son of the living God." Jesus replied, "Blessed are you, Simon son of Jonah, for this was not revealed to you by man, but by my Father in heaven."

—**MATTHEW 16:13–17**

Praise him for his revelation.

The modern electron microscope was created in 1932 when German physicists Ernst Ruska and Max Knoll constructed a prototype that used electron waves to obtain magnifications that ordinary light waves would never be able to achieve. Since then, modern improvements on that same prototype have enabled scientists to magnify an object up to two million times. Objects that have always existed can now be seen in ways never before imagined.

The objects have always been there, but until recently we never had the ability to reveal their true properties.

Peter, the other disciples, and Jesus were once walking into Caesarea Philippi, and Peter had a revelation about Jesus. Peter had been walking with Jesus for some time, but God finally gave him the ability to see Jesus' true nature. God revealed who Jesus was.

We tend to see Jesus as we see everyday objects—with our natural eyes. Have you ever seen images from an electron microscope? The minute details of even the most ordinary items suddenly become amazing, simply because we've never seen anything like it before.

If we could get a glimpse of Jesus as he really is, what would we do? We have hints, clues, and ideas about Jesus, but the actual knowledge is too overpowering, too overwhelming for us to know it completely.

Prayer for the Day:

Jesus, how much are you really worth? Do I dare ask the question? Can you even answer it? Is it answerable? Reveal yourself to me, little by little, Lord. I want to see what it really cost you on that cross. I want to know you in a deeper, more magnified way, Lord.

AMEN.

DAY 27: Your Power

In the synagogue there was a man possessed by a demon, an evil spirit. He cried out at the top of his voice, "Ha! What do you want with us, Jesus of Nazareth? Have you come to destroy us? I know who you are—the Holy One of God!" "Be quiet!" Jesus said sternly. "Come out of him!" Then the demon threw the man down before them all and came out without injuring him. All the people were amazed and said to each other, "What is this teaching? With authority and power he gives orders to evil spirits and they come out!"

—Luke 4:33–36

Praise him for his authority.

So, imagine you're there in a crowded synagogue in ancient Israel, listening to this new rabbi and his radical teachings. Suddenly some demon-possessed guy starts to shout something about this rabbi and how the rabbi is the Holy One of God. Then the rabbi suddenly commands the demon to come out, and the demon obeys him.

To reiterate: The demon obeys him.

How amazed would you be? What would you do? You don't know anything about this Jesus guy; his reputation hasn't even gotten big at this point. All you know is that this man used to be demon possessed and now he isn't. And it was because of this rabbi, Jesus of Nazareth.

He is one powerful guy.

The people who witnessed this event were struggling to comprehend what had happened. They were shocked at the power Jesus possessed.

The great thing is that he still has that power. That authority. Jesus is still the same Jesus now that he was back then. Powerful. Authoritative. The ruler over all things. Surely he has the power to overcome whatever troubles we have.

Praise him.

Prayer for the Day:

Lord Jesus, I read all the time about the miracles you performed while here on earth, and I admit that sometimes I lose my sense of wonder about them. I forget about your power, Lord. But you are powerful, and I thank you for extending that power in my direction. You blow me away, Jesus. I love you.

AMEN.

DAY 28: Your Might

All of you, clothe yourselves with humility toward one another, because, "God opposes the proud but gives grace to the humble." Humble yourselves, therefore, under God's mighty hand, that he may lift you up in due time. Cast all your anxiety on him because he cares for you.

—1 PETER 5:5–7

Praise him for his strength.

Fashion trends come and go. What was considered "cool" yesterday is "out" today, but it's only a matter of time before that outdated fashion will become stylish again.

Fashion is fickle, and one must really stay on one's toes to keep up with the revolving door of "coolness."

Perhaps that's why God instructs us to clothe ourselves with humility. Now, when this verse was written, fashion wasn't as important as it is in today's culture. But it's been said that "clothes make the man," so looking at this in a modern context, we can say that clothes do indeed make the man—or woman—and that clothing ourselves in humility instead of vanity is the way to be exalted.

Humility equals exaltation. Humility is far from fickle. Humility doesn't seek out the latest trend; it is what it is at all times. Humility is consistent.

And through our purposeful act of putting on humility, we see God's strength put on display. Our humility puts his strength into action, and at the proper time, we can see his might lift us up to where we belong.

Prayer for the Day:

God, you are so mighty. Your ways are a
mystery to me, and this whole putting-on-
humility-in-order-to-be-lifted-up thing is a
little incongruent with what I know. But I
trust you, Lord. I trust that you know what
you're talking about. And I realize that I can't
be as humble as I need to be without your help.
So help me to be humble. Help me to dress
myself in humility, so that I might please you.

AMEN.

DAY 29: Your Endless Love

For I am convinced that neither death nor life, neither angels nor demons, neither the present nor the future, nor any powers, neither height nor depth, nor anything else in all creation, will be able to separate us from the love of God that is in Christ Jesus our Lord.

—ROMANS 8:38–39

Praise him for his patience.

Stop signs. Deadlines. Guardrails. Borders. Expiration dates. Final chapters. Closing credits. Sign-offs. Sunsets.

We are surrounded by constant endings.

All around us, things are ending. Coming to a close. Being restricted.

But there is one thing surrounding us that will never end and that can never be shut out. There is no gulf to swallow it, no way to extinguish it. It is the love of God that is in Christ Jesus.

There is no end. No stop sign. No deadline. No barrier that prevents God's love from continuing on. And on. And on. And on.

There is nothing we can do to make him stop loving us. That is how persistent God is. That is how patient he is. Where we get frustrated and annoyed, he stays patient in his love.

Christ's love is endless.
It knows no boundaries.
It recognizes no borders. It sees no
ethnicities.
It just patiently carries on.

Christ's love.

Prayer for the Day:

Lord, help me to grasp even the tiniest bit of this love you have for me. Help me to internalize it. Help me take it to heart. Help me to receive this unending love. You're patient, Jesus. You're persistent. And I love you for it. I receive your love.

AMEN.

DAY 30: Then Surely They Would Never Cease to Praise

Even though I walk through the valley of the shadow of death, I will fear no evil, for you are with me; your rod and your staff, they comfort me. You prepare a table before me in the presence of my enemies. You anoint my head with oil; my cup overflows. Surely goodness and love will follow me all the days of my life, and I will dwell in the house of the LORD forever.

—PSALM 23:4–6

Praise him for who he is.

God is our Great Shepherd. Sheep don't really know what they're doing or where they're going; they're just content to munch on some grass and baa in their sheep voices. They rely on the shepherd for instruction and for guidance.

David, who wrote this psalm, was a great shepherd himself. He knew what he was doing when he compared us to the animals for which he cared. He knew how easily sheep can go astray and how easily they can get into danger. He knew how much a shepherd cared for his flock and the lengths a good shepherd would go to in order to retrieve a lost lamb.

He knew how the rod and the staff were comforts to sheep, even though they might seem restrictive. The sheep needed the direction and motivation that these two instruments provided, and the shepherd knew it, whether the sheep did or not.

God is our Great Shepherd. He knows what's best for us, even when we don't. And he knows that he is guiding us to a place of eternal pastures full of green, green grass.

We have in store for us an eternity in the house of the Lord, in service of our Great Shepherd. Surely we should never cease to praise him because of who he is.

The Shepherd.

Prayer for the Day:

Yes, Jesus, I've gone astray before. And from my sheep-perspective eyes, that rod and staff looked pretty restricting. But I see, or at least I think I see, what you're really up to. That if I trust who you are, you'll guide me to your house. I do trust who you are. I love who you are. You are my Great Shepherd. Guide me. Love me. Care for me.

AMEN.

Additional copies of this and other
Honor products are available wherever good books are sold.

Other titles in the *30 Days of Worship* series:
Here I Am to Worship
Blessed Be Your Name
In Christ Alone
The Heart of Worship
Better Is One Day

If you have enjoyed this book,
or if it has had an impact on your life,
we would like to hear from you.

Please contact us at:

Honor Books
Cook Communications Ministries, Dept. 201
4050 Lee Vance View
Colorado Springs, CO 80918

Or visit our Web site:
www.cookministries.com

HONOR ᴴᴮ BOOKS